No More Pain

I can fly!

Lisa M. Buske

ISBN-13:
978-0615943473

ISBN-10:
0615943470

Photography by Lisa M Buske
Older photos Scanned from family albums

Cover & Angel Photographs used with permission
From Janet and Kae of Criswell Embroidery & Design.

To purchase the "Awareness Angel" pattern & view others:
Embroidery design © Criswell Embroidery & Design
http://www.criswell-emb.com/index.html

A special thanks to Debra Allen for making these
Beautiful angel ornaments. Your heart is a blessing
To many ~ may you continue to inspire and encourage
Others through your sewing & embroidery.

For my younger sister, Heidi M Allen
Missing since April 3, 1994
And the friends and family who left us too soon…

Once upon a time on a cloud way up high

God looked down because He heard His child's cry

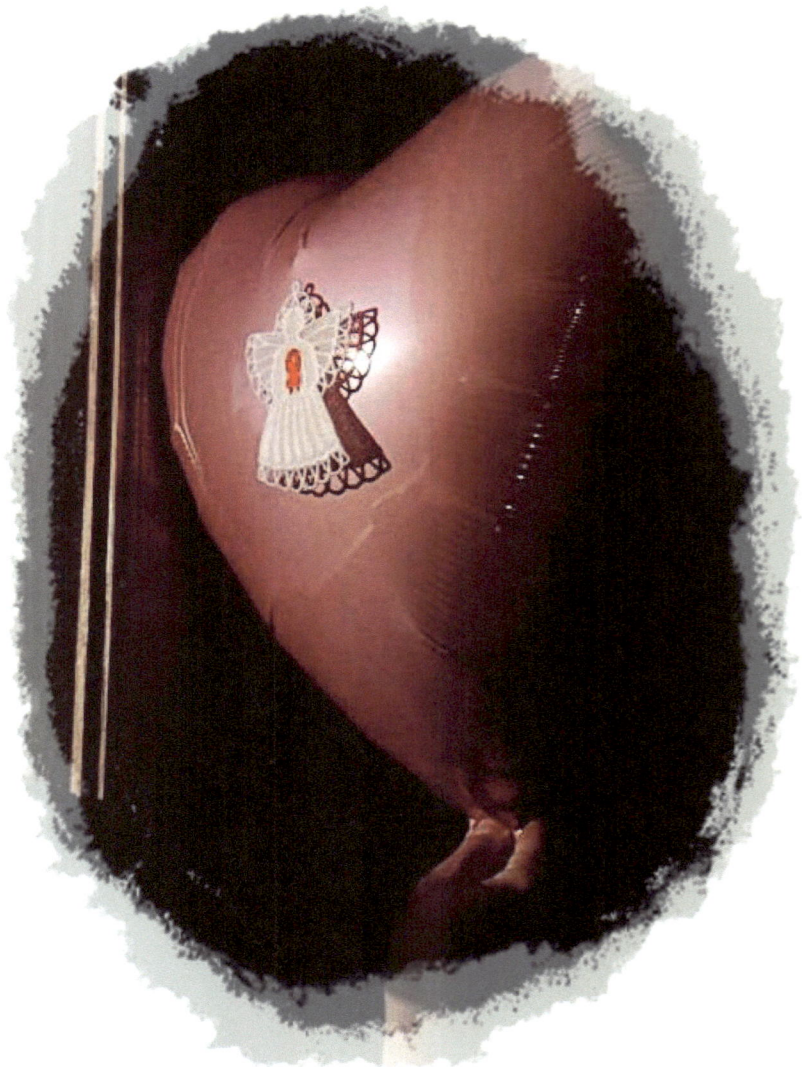

His heart ached for the fear, pain, and distress He heard,

Additional compassion and love were stirred

2011 4:07 pm

Although saddened to know His children must suffer

Not to be thought of or invited to help is even tougher

God seeks to save His hurt and lost children

Yet until asked to help, He can only listen

God separated the clouds to be a little closer

In hopes she'd lift a prayer He could answer

Her struggle, the family and friend's prayerful pleas

Brought our Heavenly Father to His knees

If only His children knew He hears each word

Listening and waiting to move them forward

God waits while she continues to fight

Hoping and praying she calls for Him tonight

Finally, she resigns to test the theory

She is too tired and her body is weary

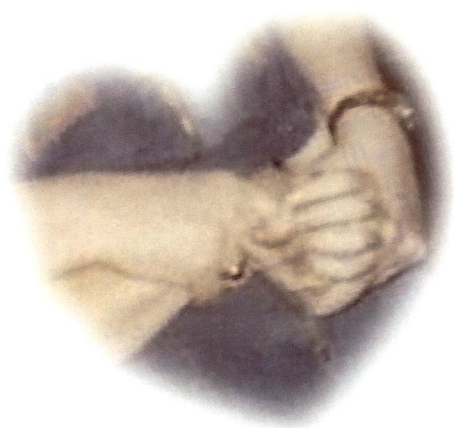

Her words, silent to those holding her hand

Yet poignant to the One living in the Promise Land

"Jesus help me" is music to God's ears

Without hesitation His saving grace appears

As she closes her eyes and accepts God's gift

His angels descend and hold her hand for the trip

Once lost...now found

Earthly pain and suffering a thing of the past

God's healing and love is unsurpassed

Rejoice – there are no tears in heaven

God holds our loved ones and all is forgiven

He welcomes them home, to a life eternal…

To live with His heavenly angels

Until we see each other again,

You must remember...

The pain is gone, once lost and now found.

I can fly!

This letter is written as if from our loved ones in heaven.
God gave me these words and today I gift them to you.
~Lisa M Buske~

To the ones I love,

I know you miss me and I miss you too
As I look down from this beautiful place
It's hard to believe we were together not so long ago

Laughing, crying, and making memories
I never planned to get sick or to leave
But God had other plans

You've done nothing wrong and all is forgiven
I send my love to you from heaven

You must know I see you each and every day
Through the clouds and God's sweet ways

I'm thankful for the time we had
Each moment a priceless treasure

Although you can't see me, I see you
Each time the sun peeks through the clouds
Know this is me looking down from above
To check on you and send some love

Instead of rushing to your next spot
Pause a moment to let the sun shine on your face
Close your eyes and remember a time
When we were once together

And remember that through Jesus
We'll be together...forever

I know you feel all the pain
But you must know it's not like that here

Once lost, now found
The pain is gone
Fear is replaced with hope
And only the good remains

I love you!

Other Books by Lisa M Buske

<u>Where's Heidi?</u>
<u>One Sister's Journey</u>
Also on Kindle
~One sister's journey following the abduction of her only sister, a journey of hope and learning to trust God again.

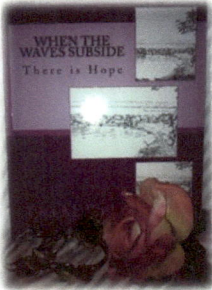

<u>When the Waves Subside</u>
<u>There is Hope</u>
Also on Kindle
~A short story to show the strength exhibited by the grieving parent

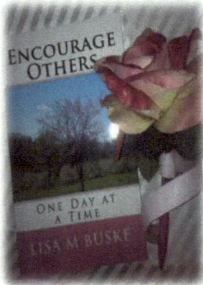

<u>Encourage Others</u>
<u>One Day at a Time</u>
~ an organizational tool to keep track of those important dates

http://LisaMBuske.com
http://www.lisambuske.com/blog.html
Email: lbuskewriter@aol.com
Twitter: @LisaBuske
Facebook: "Where's Heidi?"
Mailing: P.O. Box 261, New Haven, New York 13121

www.ingramcontent.com/pod-product-compliance
Lightning Source LLC
Chambersburg PA
CBHW040145070426
42448CB00032B/22